2588 792
CW00684452

Strength

for the Journey

One word frees us of all
the weight and pain of life:

That word is love.

Sophocles
(496 BC - 406 BC)

With grateful thanks to our editorial advisers
The Revd Dr Margaret Goodall, Methodist Homes (MHA)
Margaret Hinton
The Revd Canon Dr Judy Hunt
With special thanks to Maureen Pardoe
for all her invaluable assistance with the creation of this book

First published in 2015 by
Pictures to Share Community Interest Company,
a UK based social enterprise that publishes
illustrated books for older people.

www.picturestoshare.co.uk

ISBN 978-0-9563818-8-0

Front Cover: Madonna and Child, 1907-08 (tempera on panel) Marianne Stokes (1855-1927)
© Wolverhampton Art Gallery, West Midlands, UK / Bridgeman Images

Front endpapers: A jackdaw in a misty autumn landscape.
© Alex Saberi/National Geographic/Getty Images

Rear endpapers: A fallow deer stag resting in a misty forest in Richmond Park in autumn.
© Alex Saberi/Getty Images

Title page: Footprints in Sand © Joe Drivas/Getty Images

Strength
for the Journey

Edited by

Helen J Bate & Michelle Forster

Thank you
for the food we eat,
Thank you
for the world so sweet,

Thank you
for the birds that sing,
Thank you
God for everything.

Photograph: 1950's Child praying at dinner table
© Mary Evans / Classic Stock / H. Armstrong Roberts

Text: Traditional Grace

All things bright and beautiful

Photograph: Cat. © Laura Rabachin / Getty Images

To have and to hold

from this day forward

Photograph: Portrait of newly wed couple in car © SuperStock/Getty Images.

Text. Extract from traditional Christian marriage vows

Page 10
Photograph: Bagpiper standing next to Scottish Loch © Hugh Sitton/Corbis

Text: Extract from hymn, Amazing Grace (1779), words written
by John Newton (1725–1807)

Amazing grace!

(how sweet the sound)

That saved a wretch like me!
I once was lost, but now am found,
Was blind, but now I see.

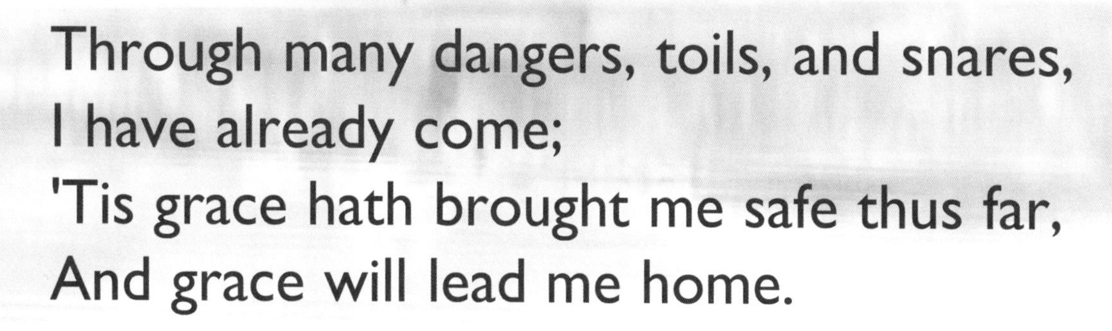

Through many dangers, toils, and snares,
I have already come;
'Tis grace hath brought me safe thus far,
And grace will lead me home.

Sunday clears away the rust of the whole week.

Painting: Communion by Carlo Frithjof Smith (1859 - 1917) © Elio Ciol/Corbis

Text: Quotation, Joseph Addison (1672 - 1719) English essayist, poet, playwright & politician

"Father I have sinned
against heaven and against you.
I am no longer worthy
to be called your son."

But the father said to his servants

"Quick! Bring the best robe
and put it on him.
Let's have a feast and celebrate,
For this son of mine
was dead and is alive again
he was lost and is found.

Luke Ch 15 v 21

Painting: Return of the Prodigal Son, 1773 (oil on canvas), Pompeo Girolamo Batoni (1708-87) / Kunsthistorisches Museum, Vienna, Austria / Bridgeman Images

That best portion of
a good man's life,

His little, nameless,
unremembered acts
of kindness
and of love.

Photograph: Grandfather with grandchild on sofa with tablet.
© Klaus Vedfelt/Getty images

Quotation: William Wordsworth, English poet (1770 - 1850)

Come to me
You who are weary
and heavy laden

And I will give you rest

Matthew Ch11 v28

Painting: Grandma's Comfort, 1883 (oil on canvas) by Frederick Brown (1851-1941) Private Collection / Photo © Christie's Images / Bridgeman Images

Our Father which art in heaven
Hallowed be thy name
Thy Kingdom come
Thy will be done
In earth as it is in heaven
Give us this day our daily bread
And forgive us our trespasses
As we forgive them that trespass against us
And lead us not into temptation
But deliver us from evil
For thine is the kingdom
The power and the glory
For ever and ever
Amen

Photograph: 1960's Two children praying at Sunday School
© Mary Evans / Classic stock / H. Armstrong Roberts

Text. The Lord's Prayer

On a hill far away
stood an old rugged cross,
The emblem of suff'ring and shame;

And I love that old cross
where the dearest and best
For a world of lost sinners was slain.

So I'll cherish the old rugged cross,
Till my trophies at last I lay down;

I will cling to the old rugged cross,
And exchange it some day for a crown.

Painting: Christ on the Cross, c.1630 (oil on canvas) by Diego Rodriguez de Silva y Velazquez (1599-1660) Prado, Madrid, Spain / Bridgeman Images

Text: From the hymn 'The Old Rugged Cross'

ΙΗΣΟΥΣ ΝΑΖΟΙΟΣ ΒΑΣΙΛΕΥΣ ΙΟΥΔΑΙΩΝ
IESVS NAZARAENVS REX IVDAEORVM

Do this
in remembrance
of me

Luke Ch 22 v19

Photograph: Communion elements - bread and wine
© Tari Faris/Getty Images

Here is the world.

Beautiful and terrible
things will happen.

Don't be afraid.

When you walk through the waters
I'll be with you.

When the fear of loneliness is looming,

Then remember
I am at your side.

Painting: A Dark Pool (oil on canvas) Laura Knight (1877-1970) Laing Art Gallery, Newcastle-upon-Tyne, UK / Tyne & Wear Archives & Museums / Bridgeman Images © Reproduced with the permission of The Estate of Dame Laura Knight DBE RA 2015 All Rights Reserved

Texts: Carl Frederick Buechner b. 1926 Ordained Presbyterian minister and author, and extract from hymn 'Do not be afraid' by Gerald Markland

We thank Thee then,
O Father,

For all things bright and good,
The seed time
and the Harvest

Our life,
our health,
our food;

Painting: In the Orchard, Haylands, Graffham (oil on canvas),
by Henry Herbert La Thangue (1859-1929) / Private Collection / Bridgeman Images

Text: Extract from traditional hymn 'We Plough the Fields and Scatter'

Away in a manger
No crib for a bed
The little Lord Jesus
Lay down his sweet head

Painting: The Little Lord Jesus Asleep on the Hay, illustration from 'The Children's Book of Hymns', 1929 (colour litho) by Cicely Mary Barker (1895-1973) Private Collection / Bridgeman Images

Text: Extract from Christmas Carol 'Away in a Manger'

Backward, turn backward,
O Time, in your flight,

Make me a child again just for tonight!

Mother, come back from the echoless shore,
Take me again to your heart as of yore;

Kiss from my forehead the furrows of care,
Smooth the few silver threads out of my hair;

Over my slumbers your loving watch keep;

Rock me to sleep, mother,
rock me to sleep!

Painting: Maternal Affection by Emile Munier (1840 - 1895)
Fine Art Photographic/Getty Images

Text: Extract from poem 'Rock Me to Sleep' by Elizabeth Chase Akers Allen
(1832 – 1911) American author, journalist and poet.

Blessed are they, who with cheery smile
stop to chat for a little while.

Blessed are they who never say,
"You've told that story twice today."

Blessed are they who know the ways
to bring back memories of yesterdays.

Blessed are they who make it known
I'm loved, respected and not alone.

Blessed are they who ease the days
of my journey home in loving ways.

Photograph: Couple standing in field, © Commerce and CultureAgency/Getty Images

Text: Extract from poem 'Friends of the Aged' written in 1958 by Esther Mary Walker (d 2005) © Curtis M Walker

They are waiting for me somewhere beyond Eden Rock:
My father, twenty-five, in the same suit
Of genuine Irish Tweed, his terrier Jack
Still two years old and trembling at his feet.

My mother, twenty three, in a sprigged dress
Drawn at the waist, ribbon in her straw hat,
Has spread the stiff white cloth over the grass.
Her hair, the colour of wheat, takes on the light.

She pours tea from a Thermos, the milk straight
From an old H.P. sauce bottle, a screw
Of paper for a cork; slowly sets out
The same three plates, the tin cups painted blue.

The sky whitens as if lit by three suns.
My mother shades her eyes and looks my way
Over the drifted stream. My father spins
A stone along the water. Leisurely,

They beckon to me from the other bank.
I hear them call, 'See where the stream-path is!
Crossing is not as hard as you might think.'

I had not thought that it would be like this.

Painting: June by George Inness,(1825 - 1894) © Brooklyn Museum/Corbis

Poem: Eden Rock by Charles Causley from Collected Poems 1951-2000 (Picador, 2000), © Estate of Charles Causley 2000, used by permission of David Higham Associates.

To every thing there is a season,
and a time to every purpose
under the heaven:

A time to be born,
and a time to die;

A time to plant,
a time to pluck up
that which is planted;

A time to weep,
and a time to laugh;

A time to mourn,
and a time to dance.

From Ecclesiastes Ch 3

Photograph: Rustic wheelbarrow in garden shed. © Tim Platt/Getty Images

The coffin of Deborah,
Dowager Duchess
of Devonshire
arrives at St Peter's Church,
in Chatsworth, England.

The Dowager
Duchess Of Devonshire
was the last surviving
Mitford sister,

and died aged 94
in 2014.

Photograph: (Photo by Dave Thompson/Getty Images)

Life's greatest
happiness
is to be convinced
we are loved.

Photograph: Mum and Baby © Kelvin Murray/Getty Images

Text: Victor Hugo, Les Miserables, 1862/French dramatist, novelist, & poet (1802 - 1885)

The miracle
is not to fly in the air,
or to walk on the water,

but to walk on the earth.

Photograph: A young woman walks through the bluebell woods in Wiltshire with her dog. © Niels van Gijn/Getty Images

Text: Chinese Proverb

May the roads rise up
to meet you,

May the wind
be always at your back,

May the sun shine
warm upon your face,

May the rains
fall soft upon fields

And until we meet again
May God hold you
in the palm of his hand.

Photograph: Bird Cupped In Human Hands,
© Education Images/UIG/Getty Images

Text: Irish Blessing. Anon

Acknowledgements

Our thanks to the many contributors who have allowed their texts or imagery to be used for a reduced or no fee. Every effort has been made to contact copyright holders. If you own the copyright for work that is represented, but have not been contacted, please get in touch via our website.

Many thanks to our sponsors, without whose financial support this book would not have been created.

The Mustard Seeds Awards (A partnership between the Cinnamon Network & the Christian Initiative Trust)

The Elise Pilkington Charitable Trust

The Beatrice Laing Trust

All rights reserved. No part of this publication may be transmitted in any form or by any means, electronic or mechanical, including photocopying, recording or any storage and retrieval system, without the prior permission in writing from the publisher.

Published by
Pictures to Share Community Interest Company.
Tattenhall, Cheshire
www.picturestoshare.co.uk

Graphics by Duncan Watts

Printed in England by Langham Press,
Station Road, Foxton, Cambridgeshire CB22 6SA

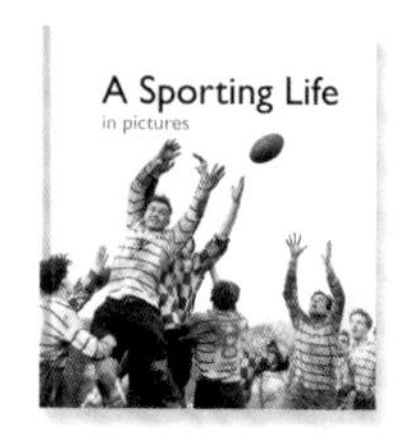

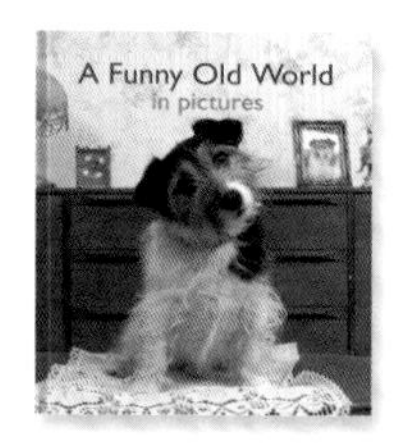

To see our other titles go to
www.picturestoshare.co.uk